11+
exam preparation and practice

Maths
Test Papers

7 - 8 years

Vino Thava
Managing Director / Founder, Three Dots Group Ltd

Dr. Krithikka Thava

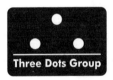

A Publication
Three Dots Centre of Excellence

Copyright warning

First edition : 2018
ISBN : 978-1-911401-02-5

Three Dots Centre of Excellence & Publication
No:26 Woodend Gardens,
Northolt, UB5 4QJ
U.K.

Email : info@threedotsgroup.co.uk
Visit our website : www.threedotsgroup.co.uk

OVERVIEW

BOOK 3 (7-8 years)

⚫ Every level book covers the sheer routine of material and practice to cover the ground.

⚫ Each paper set with 40 questions of 40 marks will have a clear mix of numerical reasoning, mental arithmetic and mathematical fluency intended to bloom child as **'Heuristic'.**

Each Test paper provide

⚫ Practice, enhance understanding and familiarise themselves with the key numerical principles.

⚫ Exercises in varied formats to focus on problem solving and critical thinking.

⚫ Employs revisiting basic concepts repeatedly, at a higher level each time.

⚫ Designed also to challenge and fun through **'mental maths'.**

How to manage child's practice

⚫ Book holds 20 test papers each with 40 marks and answers given in page **v** to **x**.

⚫ Answers to be written in Standard write in format - **box** or **line** will be given.

⚫ Expected to finish each paper by 50 minutes.

⚫ Assign every **total marks** at the end of each paper.

⚫ Take down the total marks of each test paper in the **Progress chart** at the **inner back cover** and track the child's performance.

⚫ Children need to exceed upon 85%.

Other resource

⚫ The brief of keywords given in **Search box** at the page **iv**.

⚫ **Definitions** on basic mathematics under *Know it* in between test papers.

Search box

Add or Sum	-	The total by combining two or more numbers. **e.g.** $5 + 3 = 8$
Average	-	The middle calculated value in a set of numbers.
Circle	-	A 2D curve which has all points equidistant from centre.
Corner or vertex	-	A point where two or more lines meet.
Cylinder	-	A 3D solid with 2 circular surfaces either end and a curved surface in middle.
Denominator	-	The total number of equal parts in a whole.
Difference	-	The result of subtraction. **e.g.** The difference of 5 and 2 is $5 - 2 = 3$
Double	-	To make twice a number or expression. **e.g.** double of 4 is $4 + 4 = 8$
Edge	-	The line at which two surfaces of a solid meet.
Expanded form	-	Writing a number with the sum of place values of each digit. **e.g.** $983 = 900 + 80 + 3$
Face value	-	The value of digit in a number.
Factors	-	A list of numbers which can divide the given number with no remainder. **e.g.** 1, 2 and 3 are the factors of 6
Even	-	A number divisible by 2. **e.g.** 2, 4, 6, ...
Equal	-	The identical or same measure, quantity or a value.
Face	-	A flat surface in a shape or solid.
Line of symmetry	-	A line that divides the figure or shape into two identical parts.
Mirror line	-	The axis of symmetry in a figure or shape.
Nearest	-	A value close to the exact number.
Numerator	-	A number of equal parts taken from a whole.
Odd	-	A number not divisible by 2. **e.g.** 1, 3, 5, ...
Perimeter	-	The total length of line segments in a 2D shape.
Prime number	-	A whole number divisible by one and itself. **e.g.** 2, 3, 5, 7 ...
Rectangle	-	A flat four-sided equiangular shape with 2 long sides & 2 short sides opposite to each other.
Rectangular number	-	The numbers that can make a rectangular dot pattern. **e.g.** 4, 6, 8, 9, 10 ....
Round up	-	A number rounded to a higher number.
Sphere	-	A 3D round solid completely symmetrical around its centre.
Square	-	A flat four-sided equiangular shape with equal sides.
Subtract	-	To remove a number or object from another. **e.g.** $5 - 3 = 2$
Tens	-	The second digit from the right of a whole number. **e.g.** 8 tens in 983
Triangle	-	A flat shape with three sides and three vertices.
Thousands	-	The fourth digit from the right of a whole number. **e.g.** 4 thousands in 64568
Triangular number	-	A number that can make a triangular dot pattern. **e.g.** 1, 3, 6, 10 ...
Triple	-	To make thrice or three times a number. **e.g.** triple of 5 is $5 + 5 + 5 = 15$
Units/Ones	-	The rightmost digit of a whole number. **e.g.** 9 units in 19
Venn Diagram	-	A diagram that groups different sets of elements.

TEST PAPER 1

Date ....

Find how many **corners** and **sides** each has:

1-2  _____6_____ **corners** _____6_____ **sides**

3-4 _____0_____ **corners** _____1_____ **sides**

Draw the **next pattern.**

5

6

7 50 **more than** 246 is _____296_____

8 50 **less than** 321 is _____271_____

9 69 **nearest to 10** is _____70_____

10 75 **nearest to 10** is _____80_____

11 84 **nearest to 10** is _____80_____

12 23 **nearest to 10** is _____20_____

The table shows the number of students who were absent in a day of a week. ☺ = 2 student

Monday	☺ ☺ ☺
Tuesday	☺
Wednesday	☺ ☺ ☺ ☺
Thursday	———————
Friday	☺ ☺ ☺ ☺ ☺

13 On which day, all the students were present? ___Thursday___

14 On which day, most number of students were absent? ___Friday___

15 How many students were absent on Wednesday? ___8___

16 On which day, exactly 6 students were absent? ___Monday___

17 How many absence were marked altogether on Wednesday and Friday?

___18___

18 How many **more** students were absent on Friday than Tuesday?

___8___

19 **Total** number of absence marked in the whole week ___26___

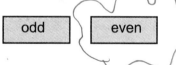

20 Ring the **smallest** number.

216	162	126	612	621

21 Tick (✓) the correct one.

The number ending with 0, 2, 4, 6, 8 is | odd | | even |

Observe the patterns and fill in the blank box.

22-23

4	9	14	19	24	29	34	39	44

24-25

6	10	20	30	40	50	60	70	80

26-27

K	V	M	K	V	M	K	V	M

28-29   500 ml + 500 ml = $\boxed{1000}$ ml = $\boxed{1}$ l

30-31   1250 g + 750 g = $\boxed{2000}$ g = $\boxed{2}$ kg

Write the answer.

32   16 - 10 = $\boxed{46}$ **33**   16 + $\boxed{3}$ = 19

34   29 - 9 = $\boxed{20}$ **35**   29 + $\boxed{1}$ = 30

36   9 x 4 = $\boxed{36}$ **37**   30 ÷ $\boxed{5}$ = 6

38   10 x 9 = $\boxed{90}$ **39**   20 ÷ $\boxed{4}$ = 5

40   Tick (✓) the correct one.

(125 : 152)   (983 : 938)   (586 : 568)   (981 : ?)

181	918	981	819

6

2

2

8

1

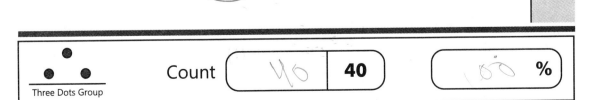

Count   40   40   00 %

Three Dots Group

3

Date ....

The table shows the favourite ice-cream flavour of children in **Class III**.

Ice-Cream Flavour		Number of Children
Pineapple	**P**	5
Butterscotch	**B**	6
Strawberry	**S**	8
Chocolate	**C**	10
Vanilla	**V**	6

e.g. In the class, 5 children like _____**P**_____

1 The **most** popular flavour is ___Chocolate___

2 The **least** popular flavour is ___Pineapple___

3 ___4___ **more** children like chocolate than vanilla.

4 ___Vanilla___ and ___Butterscotch___ flavours are **equally** liked.

5 How many children like strawberry? ___8___

6 Altogether how many children like **P** and **V** ? ___11___

7 **Total** number of children in Class III is ___25___

7

Jack lives **200 m** from Tim's house. Pin lives **150 m** from Tim's house in opposite direction.

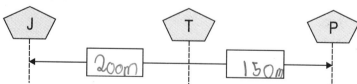

8-9 Fill the correct distance in the boxes.

10 How far did Pin live from Jack's house? ___350 m___

11 If Jack and Pin started walking at same time with same speed towards Tim's house, who will reach 1st ? ___Pin___

4

12   59 round to **nearest 10** is   _60_

13   73 round to **nearest 10** is   _70_   44

14   88 round to **nearest 10** is   _90_

15   265 round to **nearest 100** is   _300_

16   154 round to **nearest 100** is   _200_

17   How many **9s** are there in 45?   _5_

18   80 **add** 25 equals   _105_

19   80 **multiplied** by 3 equals   _240_

20   80 **divided** by 2 equals   _40_

21   80 **subtract** 30 equals   _50_

22   How many **10s** are there in 190?   _19_

23   How many **10s** are there in 240?   _24_

24   How many **4s** are there in 28?   _7_

25   A new building is **24 m** high and the old building is **15 m** high. How much higher is the new building? _9m_

There are 240 books in a study room.

26   How many are not story books?   _190_

27   Estimate the number of shelves.   _12_

28   How many books are covered?   _115_

- Each shelf has 20 books
- 60 books are story books
- 25 books need covers

Write the time using **am** or **pm.**

29   Quarter past 7 in the morning   _7:15 ~~7:15 am~~_

30   Quarter to 6 in the evening   _5:45pm_

Cross (x) the odd one out.

31

3	5	7	11	~~15~~

32

6	8	~~21~~	22	30

13

1

3

2

2

33
| shirt | trouser | vest | tie | ring |

(ring circled)

Write the **greatest** and **smallest** 3-digit number using the digits 3, 9 and 5.

34 Greatest | 9 | 5 | 3 | **35** Smallest | 3 | 5 | 9 |

Tick (✓) the correct one.

36

| Umpire : Match | | Students : ? |

| Court | Temple | Class | Lawyer |

(Class circled)

37

| 1 : 23 | 4 : 56 | 3 : 45 | 7 : ? |

| 89 | 98 | 65 | 32 |

(89 circled)

38 **Half** of 80 = | 40 | **39** **Double** 25 = | 50 |

40 Tim is the **5ᵗʰ** man from the left and **6ᵗʰ** man from the right in a row. How many men are there in the row? | 10 |

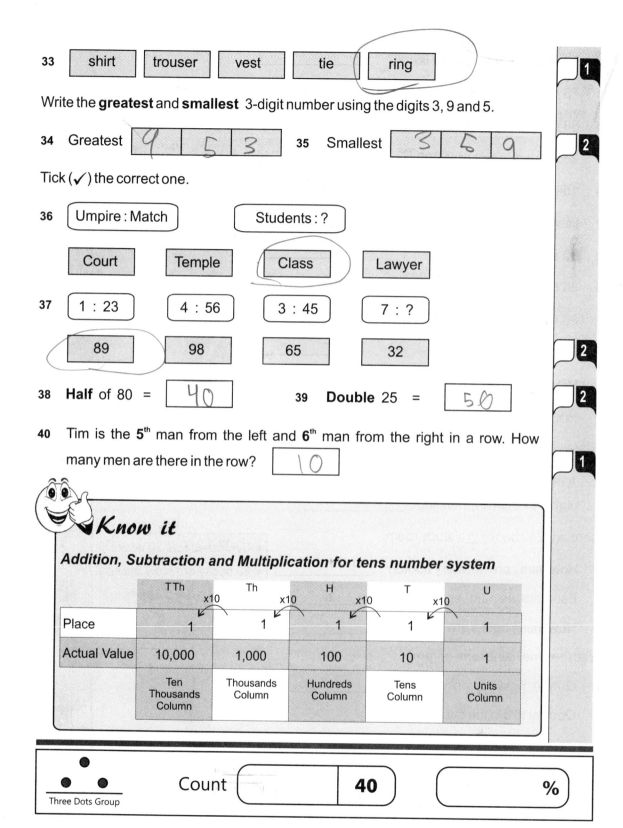

Know it

Addition, Subtraction and Multiplication for tens number system

	TTh	Th	H	T	U
	x10	x10	x10	x10	
Place	1	1	1	1	1
Actual Value	10,000	1,000	100	10	1
	Ten Thousands Column	Thousands Column	Hundreds Column	Tens Column	Units Column

Three Dots Group

Count | 40 | | % |

Tick (✓) the series on ⬚I if **increasing** order or on ⬚D if **decreasing** order.

◯ Ring the **greatest** number and ⬚ Box the **smallest** number.

e.g.	10	11	12	13	(14)	I✓	D
1-3	(16)	14	12	10	8	I	(D)
4-6	(90)	95	100	105	110	(I)	D
7-9	(987)	897	879	798	789	I	(D)
10-12	3	6	9	12	15	(I)	D

12

Use the **signs** in the boxes.

e.g.	3 **greater than** 2,	3 > 2
	4 **less than** 6,	4 < 6
	5 **equals** 5,	5 = 5

13 99 [>] 9   **14** 109 [=] 119

15 10 [<] 0   **16** 201 [=] 210

17 26 + 4 [>] 30   **18** 16 x 2 [>] 32

19 6 x 5 [<] 20   **20** 30 ÷ 2 [<] 25

8

Look at the shape.

21 How many **circles** are there? _____6_____

22 How many **triangles** are there? _____2_____

Tick (✓) the correct one.

2

23 The numbers ending with 1, 3, 5, 7, 9 is [even] (odd)

24 £2 = [20p] (200p) 2000p [2p] [4p]

2

7

25	5 kg	=	5 g	50 g	10 g	500 g	5000 g
26	1 l 20 ml	=	120 ml	102 ml	1020 ml	1200 ml	1002 ml
27	3 m	=	30 cm	30 mm	300 cm	300 mm	3000 cm

28 Taking **50** from **300** gives ___250___

29 Adding 5 **hundreds** to 4 **tens** gives 540

30 **Round up** 387 to the nearest **ten**. ___390___

Cross (x) the odd one out.

31	5	9	15	21	26

32	1A	2B	3C	4P	5E

33 △ □ ○ ◇ ⬡

Tick (✓) the correct one in the box to complete the pattern.

34

16 (8) 2	24 (6) 4	15 (3) 5	40 (?) 4
4	40	10	8

35

1:2	2:4	4:8	8:?
16	2	1	8

36

10A	30C	50E	?
60F	70F	70G	40G

Write the answer.

37 **Half** of 78 = 39

38 **Double** 15 = 30

39 5^2 = 5 x 5 = 25

40 6^2 = 6 x 6 = 36

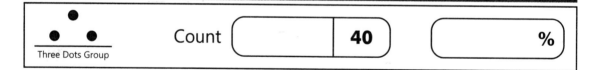

Three Dots Group   Count | **40**   %

The table shows favourite fruits of **class III** students.

Write the **symbol** or **number** in the space.

Favourite Fruit	Symbol	Number of students
Pear	**P**	7
Apple	**A**	4
Orange	**O**	2
Pineapple	**Pa**	3
Banana	**B**	6
Mango	**M**	8

1 Which is the **most** favourite fruit? _____ M

2 Which is the **least** favourite fruit? _____ O

3 How many **more** students like mango than orange? _____ 6

4 How many students like pears? _____ 7

5 **Total** number of students who like pears and apple _____ 11

6 How many students like banana than pineapple? _____ 3

7 **Total** number of students in the class _____ 30

Write the answer.

8 $27 + 5 = 27 + 3 + 2 =$ _____ 32

9 $66 + 14 = 66 + 4 + 10 =$ _____ 80

10 $52 + 18 = 52 + 8 + 10 =$ _____ 70

7

3

11 48 + 52 = 48 + 2 + 50 = ___100___

12 99 + 11 = 99 + 1 + 10 = ___110___

Colour to show the **Fraction.**

13 $\frac{3}{4}$ ☐   **14** $\frac{2}{5}$

15 In a wall clock, minute hand on **12** and hour hand on **4**. Then the

     time is ___4___ **O'clock**

16-17 The clock shows **11 O'clock**, minute hand on ___12___ and hour

     hand on ___11___

18-19 The clock shows **12 O'clock**, minute hand on ___12___ and hour

     hand on ___12___

20 The clock shows minute hand on **12** and hour hand on **3**. The **angle**

     between both hands ___90°___

Arrange in columns and **add**:

e.g. 13 + 27

T	O
1	3
+ 2	7
4	0

21 22 + 23

T	O
2	2
+ 2	3
4	5

22 18 + 26

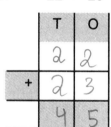

T	O
2	6
+ 1	8
4	4

23 29 + 30

T	O
3	0
+ 2	9
5	9

24 37 + 30

T	O
3	0
+ 3	7
6	7

25 49 + 25

T	O
4	9
+ 2	5
7	4

Write the answers.

26 16 ÷ 4 = [4]

27 30 ÷ 6 = [5]

28 75 ÷ 5 = [15]

29 6 x 7 = [42]

30 9 x 9 = [81]

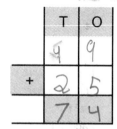

2

2

6

5

5

Tick (✓) the correct one.

31 The **smallest** natural **number**

| 0 | 1 ✓ | 10 | 9 |

32 Number of zeros in one thousand

| 4 | 5 | 3 ✓ | 6 |

33 **Product** of 5 and x is written as

| $x + 5$ | $x\,5$ | $5x$ ✓ | $x - 5$ |

34 Number of days in 3 weeks

| 15 | 18 | 21 ✓ | 24 |

35 **Expanded form** of 1983 is 1000 + 900 + ? + 3

| 8 | 80 ✓ | 800 | 8000 |

36 The difference between **place values** of 9 and 8 in the number 1981

| 1 | 900 | 820 ✓ | 980 |

Write the answer.

37 19 + [11] = 30

38 200 ÷ [8] = 25

39 20 x [4] = 80

40 100 ÷ [5] = 20

6

4

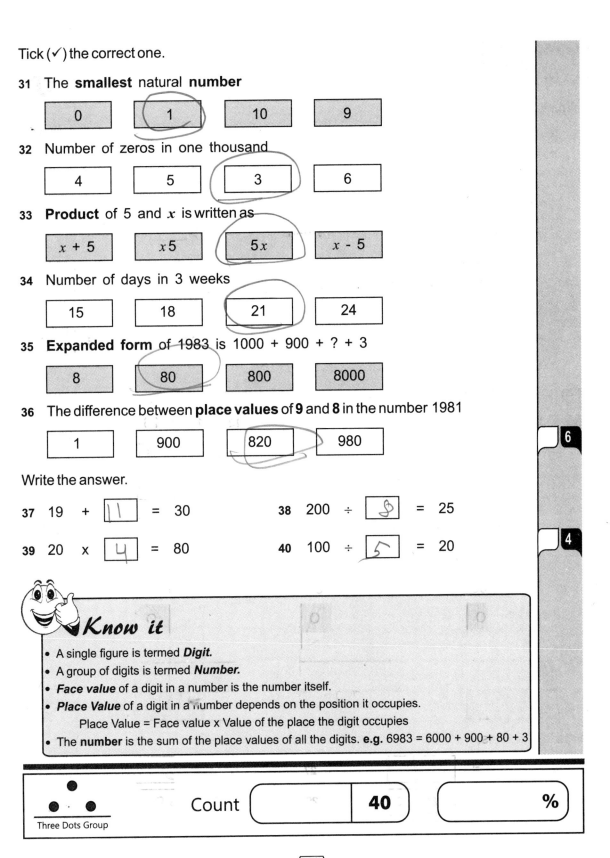

Know it

- A single figure is termed **Digit**.
- A group of digits is termed **Number**.
- **Face value** of a digit in a number is the number itself.
- **Place Value** of a digit in a number depends on the position it occupies.
    Place Value = Face value x Value of the place the digit occupies
- The **number** is the sum of the place values of all the digits. **e.g.** 6983 = 6000 + 900 + 80 + 3

Three Dots Group

Count | **40** | %

The list shows the number of hours 5 children watch television in a weekend.

Name	Hours in a day		Total hours
	Saturday	Sunday	
Mane	1	1	2
Hane	2	2	4
Sam	0	3	3
Jim	2	2	4
Jake	2	4	6

1-5   Fill in the **total** column.

6-7   Name the children who watch same hours   _Hane ⁴Jim_

8   Who watch the TV **most**?   _³Jake_

9   Who did not watch TV on Saturday?   _Sam_

10   Who spent the **most** time on Sunday?   _⁶Jake_

11   **Total** hours spent on watching TV by the 5 children   _19 hours_

12-21 Shade the minutes that have passed and write the time.

e.g.

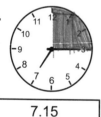

| 7.15 |

12-13

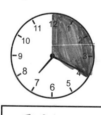

| 7:20 |

14-15

| 10:10 |

16-17

| 8.25 |

18-19

| 9:35 |

20-21

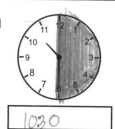

| 1030 |

22 The jug holds **1 litre** and the glass holds **200 ml**. How many glasses of milk
    should fill the jug? ___5___

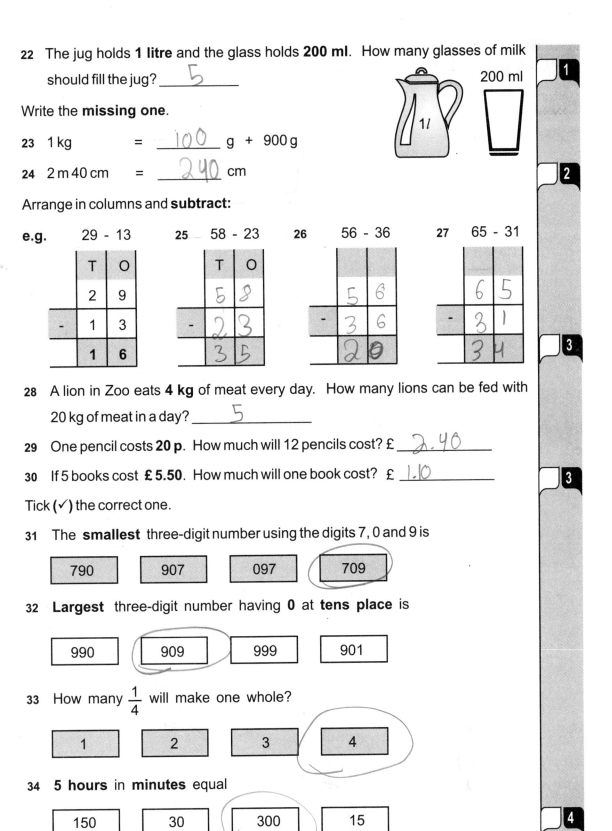

200 ml

1ℓ

Write the **missing one**.

23 1 kg   = ___100___ g + 900 g

24 2 m 40 cm   = ___240___ cm

Arrange in columns and **subtract**:

e.g.   29 - 13   25   58 - 23   26   56 - 36   27   65 - 31

T	O
2	9
- 1	3
1	6

T	O
5	8
- 2	3
3	5

5	6
- 3	6
2	0

6	5
- 3	1
3	4

28 A lion in Zoo eats **4 kg** of meat every day. How many lions can be fed with
    20 kg of meat in a day? ___5___

29 One pencil costs **20 p**. How much will 12 pencils cost? £ ___2.40___

30 If 5 books cost **£ 5.50**. How much will one book cost? £ ___1.10___

Tick (✓) the correct one.

31 The **smallest** three-digit number using the digits 7, 0 and 9 is

| 790 | 907 | 097 | (709) |

32 **Largest** three-digit number having **0** at **tens place** is

| 990 | (909) | 999 | 901 |

33 How many $\frac{1}{4}$ will make one whole?

| 1 | 2 | 3 | (4) |

34 **5 hours** in **minutes** equal

| 150 | 30 | (300) | 15 |

35 1000 times **1 metre** equal

| 1 cm | 100 cm | 10 km | 1 km |

36 Number of weeks in a year

| 52 | 48 | 54 | 50 |

Write the answer.

37 The **average** of **17** and **21** is ___19___

38 Number of fives in 100 equal ___20___

39 **4** and **3** are a pair of **factors** of ___12___

40 Round 92 to the **nearest 10** ___90___

2

4

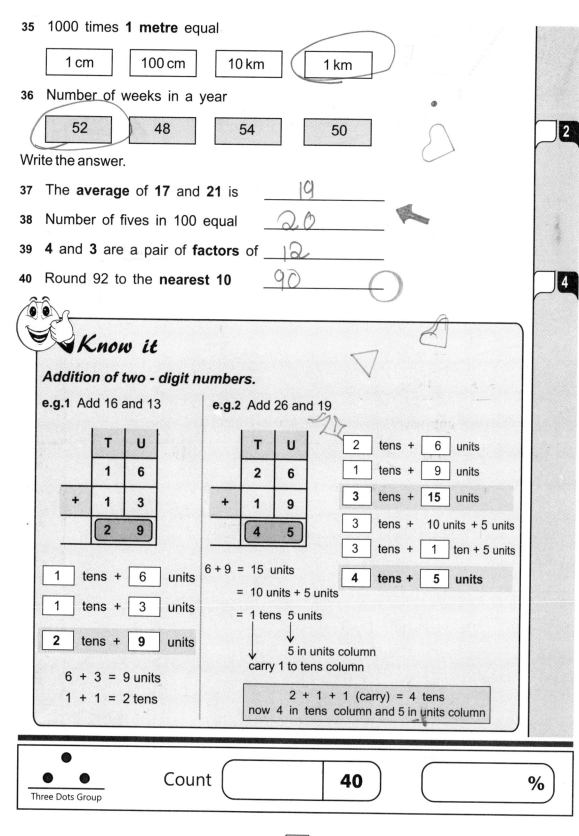

Know it

Addition of two - digit numbers.

e.g.1 Add 16 and 13

T	U
1	6
+ 1	3
2	**9**

1	tens +	6	units
1	tens +	3	units
2	tens +	**9**	units

6 + 3 = 9 units
1 + 1 = 2 tens

e.g.2 Add 26 and 19

T	U
2	6
+ 1	9
4	**5**

2	tens +	6	units
1	tens +	9	units
3	tens +	15	units
3	tens +	10 units + 5 units
3	tens +	1	ten + 5 units
4	**tens +**	**5**	**units**

6 + 9 = 15 units
  = 10 units + 5 units
  = 1 tens 5 units

5 in units column
carry 1 to tens column

2 + 1 + 1 (carry) = 4 tens
now 4 in tens column and 5 in units column

Count | 40 | %

Three Dots Group

The milkshake recipe is given. Quantitate the amount for a full recipe and a half recipe.

| 1 bottle = 400 ml, | 1 cup = 220 ml, | 1 table spoon = 40 ml |

	Ingredients for full recipe	Full recipe	Half recipe
e.g.	3 cups strawberry squash	660 ml	330 ml
1-2	3 cups vanilla ice-cream	660 l	330
3-4	2 cups milk	440	220
5-6	2 bottles strawberry juice	800 mL	400 ml
7-8	3 tablespoons honey	120 mL	60 ml

8

9   Ring the ingredients which are **equal** in amount.

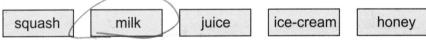

| squash | milk | juice | ice-cream | honey |

10   Ring the ingredient which is **least** in amount.

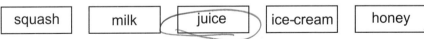

| squash | milk | juice | ice-cream | honey |

2

Write the **missing one.**

11	48	44	40	36	32	28
12	5A	8B	11C	14D	17E	20F
13	100z	90y	80x	70w	60v	____
14	2ab	4bc	6cd	8de	10ef	12fg

4

15   Adam's younger sister goes to school. Her age could be ___?___ Tick (✓)

| 9 months | 60 years | 10 years | 1 year | 10 months |

1

15

Write the answer.

e.g. 6 x 5

	T	O
		6
x		5
	3	0

16 7 x 6

	T	O
		7
x		6
	4	2

17 9 x 3

	T	O
		9
x		3
	2	7

Write the answer.

e.g. 76 = __7__ **tens** + __6__ **units**

18-19 84 = __8__ **tens** + __4__ **units**

20-21 97 = __9__ **tens** + __7__ **units**

22 If you **add** me to myself, you get **20**. Who am I? __10__

23 If you **add** me to myself and add 8, you get **30**. Who am I? __11__ __11__

24 If you **double** myself, you get **30**. Who am I? __15__

25 If you **add** me to **6 units**, you get **46**. Who am I? __40__

26 My **units** digit is **4**. My **tens** digit is **2** more than my units digit.

Who am I? __264__

Put the sign **>** , **<** **or** **=** in the space.

27 29 __>__ 19

28 35 + 5 __=__ 30 + 10

29 33 __<__ 43

30 3 **tens** __>__ 2 **tens**

Tick (✓) the correct one.

31 Which number has 5 in **tens place**?

567	657	765	705

32 What is the **place value** of 2 in the number 4275?

2	20	200	2000

2

4

5

4

2

33 The value of $(10 \div 2) + (50 + 5) = $ **30** x **?**

| 5 | 4 | 2 | 10 |

34 The **triangular number** shown in pattern is

| 3 | 5 | 4 | 6 |

35-36 A game started at **4.30 pm** and ended at **6.40 pm.** How long was the game? _____ 1 _____ hr _____ 10 _____ min

Write the answer.

37 Reduce 15 by 5 = 10

38 5^2 = 25

39 Reduce 10 by 2 = 8

40 6^2 = 36

Addition of three - digit numbers.

e.g. Add 183 and 784

H	T	U
1	8	3
+ 7	8	4
		7

H	T	U
1	8	3
+ 7	8	4
	6	7

H	T	U
1	8	3
+ 7	8	4
9	6	7

Step 1 : Add units

3 + 4 = 7 units

Write 7 in units column

Step 2 : Add tens

8 + 8 = 16 tens

= 10 tens + 6 tens

= 1 hundred + 6 tens

Write 6 in tens column and

carry 1 to hundreds column

Step 3 : Add hundreds

1 + 7 + 1 (carry) = 9

Write 9 in hundreds column

Three Dots Group

Count | **40** | %

Look at the table and complete it.

	Length of wire	Cut into length	Number of pieces
e.g.	90 cm	9 cm	10
1	100 cm	2 cm	50
2	80 cm	4 cm	20
3		14 cm	2
4	_____	6 cm	4
5	60 cm	_____	5
6	70 cm	_____	2
7	50 cm	10 cm	5

7

Ring the answer.

8	$39 + 41$	=	40	60	70	(80)	100
9	$19 + 11 + 10$	=	10	15	30	35	(40)
10	$49 - 19$	=	29	39	(30)	40	68
11	$1\text{ m }20\text{ cm} - 40\text{ cm}$	=	1 m	8 m	(80 cm)	16 cm	60 cm
12	$\frac{1}{4}$ of 100	=	20	(25)	40	50	400
13	$\frac{1}{2}$ of 24	=	48	(12)	6	96	26
14	$\frac{1}{2}$ of £1.00	=	20p	2p	(50p)	100p	200p
15	**Double** 50p	=	25p	10p	(£1)	£2	50p

8

Build the **greatest** and **smallest** three digit number.

	Digits	Greatest number	Smallest number
e.g.	4, 0, 8	840	408
16-17	2, 7, 9	972	279
18-19	4, 9, 0	940	409
20-21	0, 1, 8	810	108

6

Write the **number name.**

e.g.	431	**Four hundred and thirty one**
22	635	Six hundred and thirty-five
23	506	five hundred and six
24	890	eight hundred and nitty
25	305	three hundred and five

Write the answer.

26 One **more** than 299 is _____ 300

27 One **less** than 500 is _____ 499

28 20 students have borrowed 4 books each from the library. How many books have been borrowed in all? _____

Draw the **lines** of **symmetry.**

29

30

Tick (✓) the correct one.

31 Which number has 6 in **hundreds place**?

7645	7465	6745	7456

32 One less than **greatest** three digit number

999	998	989	899

33 What **fraction** of a day is 12 hours?

$\frac{1}{4}$	$\frac{1}{3}$	$\frac{1}{2}$	$\frac{1}{5}$

34 Better **unit** to measure length of a £20 note.

m	cm	km	kg

35 Write five thousand and sixty two in **figures**. _____

4

3

2

4

1

19

Cross the correct one.

36 Is 6 a **rectangular number** ?

Yes   No

37 Is 9 a **prime** number?

Yes   No

38 Is 990 a three digit **greatest number**?

Yes   No

3

Write the answer.

39 400 ÷ 25 =   16   40 25 x 5 =   125

2

Know it

Subtraction of three - digit numbers.

e.g. Subtract 594 from 983

H	T	U
	7	13
9	8̸	3̸

	H	T	U
−	5	9	4
			9

H	T	U
8	17	13
9̸	8̸	3̸

	H	T	U
−	5	9	4
		8	9

H	T	U
8	17	13
9̸	8̸	3̸

	H	T	U
−	5	9	4
	3	8	9

Step 1 : Subtract units

3 - 4 not possible
Rearrange 8 tens
into 7 tens + 10 units
we have 10 + 3 = 13 units
in the units column.
now 13 - 4 = 9
Write 9 in units column

Step 2 : Subtract tens

7 - 9 not possible
Rearrange 9 hundreds
into 8 hundreds + 10 tens
we have 10 + 7 = 17 tens
in the tens column.
now 17 - 9 = 8
Write 8 in tens column

Step 3 : Subtract hundreds

8 - 5 = 3
Write 3 in
hundreds column

Three Dots Group

Count   **40**   %

20

Write the number of **faces, edges** and **vertices.**

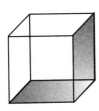  

1-3 Faces	6	1	2
4-6 Edges	8 or 12	1 or 2	1
7-9 Vertices	12 or 8	2 or 1	1

Look at the Venn diagram.

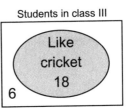

Students in class III

10 Number of students who like cricket ___18___

11 Number of students who unlike cricket ___6___

12 Number of students in the class ___24___

Write in **figures.**

13 Three hundred and thirty three ___333___

14 Nine hundred and five ___905___

15 How many **hundreds** are there in 842? ___8___

16 Benny counted **18** rail road cars in a train. 18 is **nearest** to ___20___

Ring the correct number which should be in the box.

17 30 − 20 > [ ] ⭕5 10 15 20

18 15 + 25 < [ ] 40 ⭕49 25 19

19 55 + 15 = [ ] 20 ⭕70 30 40

20 $\frac{1}{2}$ of 50 = $\frac{1}{4}$ of 100 = [ ] 60 100 160 ⭕25

9
3
2
2
4

21 **Sum** of **largest** and **smallest** two digit number is ___9+8___

22 The **difference** of **largest** and **smallest** two digit number is ___9-1___

Write the **missing one**.

23 10   A   12   B   14   C   16   D   _18_

24 C   5   D   8   E   11   _F_   14   G

25 1x2   2x3   3x4   _4x5_   5 x 6   6 x 7

26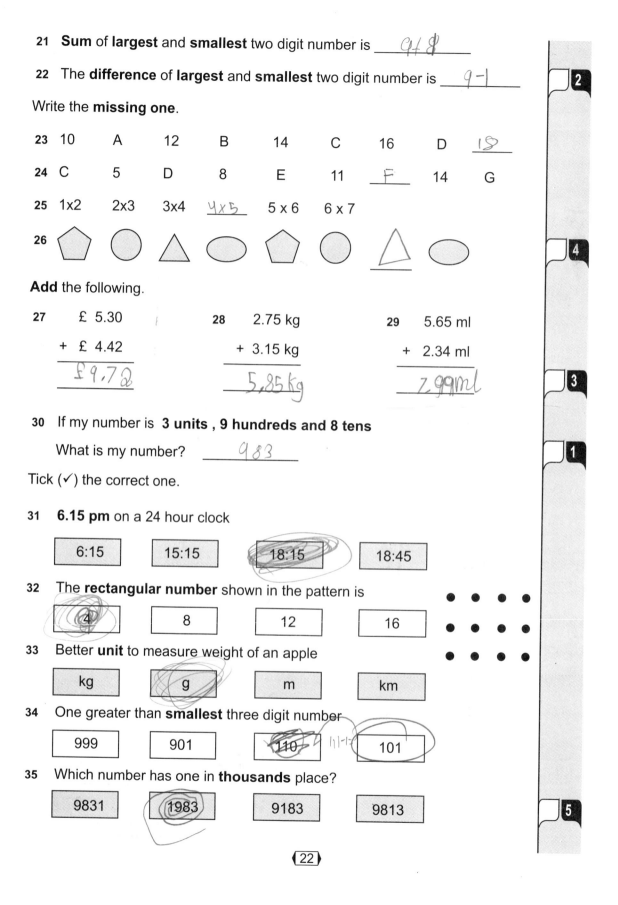

Add the following.

27   £ 5.30   28   2.75 kg   29   5.65 ml

  + £ 4.42   + 3.15 kg   + 2.34 ml
  _____   _____   _____
    £9.72   5.85 kg   7.99 ml

30 If my number is **3 units , 9 hundreds and 8 tens**

What is my number?   ___983___

Tick (✓) the correct one.

31 **6.15 pm** on a 24 hour clock

| 6:15 | 15:15 | 18:15 | 18:45 |

32 The **rectangular number** shown in the pattern is

| 4 | 8 | 12 | 16 |

33 Better **unit** to measure weight of an apple

| kg | g | m | km |

34 One greater than **smallest** three digit number

| 999 | 901 | 110 | 101 |

35 Which number has one in **thousands** place?

| 9831 | 1983 | 9183 | 9813 |

36 Write six thousand and twenty three in **figures** _____

60 22

Write the answer.

37 600 + 30 + 2 = | 632 |

38 50 x 4 = | 800 |

39 500 + 0 + 9 = | 509 |

40 15 x 15 = | 225 |

2 15
x 15
75
+ 1 50
225

Know it

Multiplication by column method

e.g.1 Multiply 32 by 3

Method 1

T	U
3	2
x	3
	6
+ 9	0
9	6

6 → 2 units x 3 = 6 units

9 0 → 3 tens x 3 = 9 tens
= 90

Step 1 - Multiply the units
Step 2 - Multiply the tens
Step 3 - Add the products

Method 2

T	U		T	U
3	2		3	2
x	3		x	3
	6		9	6

Step 1 - Multiply the units 3 x 2 = 6
Write 6 in units column

Step 2 - Multiply the tens 3 x 3 = 9
Write 9 in tens column

Note:

32   x   3   =   96
Multiplicand x Multiplier = Product

e.g.2 Multiply 234 by 21

Th	H	T	U
	2	3	4
		2	1
	2	3	4
+ 4	6	8	0
4	9	1	4

234 x 1 = 234
234 x 20 = 4680

Step 1 : Multiply the units
Write 1 x 234 = 234

Step 2 : Multiply the tens
Put 0 in units column
Write 2 x 234 = 468
Start 8 in tens column

Step 3 : Add the products

Three Dots Group

Count | **40** | %

〈23〉

The Venn diagram shows a survey taken by coach Menon about 10 students A to J.

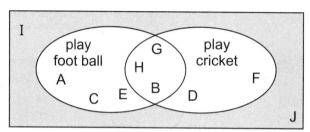

1 How many students play football?   *6*

2 How many students play cricket?   *5*

3 Who play both the sports?   *G, H, B*

4 Who neither play football nor cricket?   *I, J*

5 Who play only cricket?   *D, F*

6 Who play only football?   *A, C, E*

7 What fraction of students play cricket?   *$\frac{1}{2}$ or $\frac{5}{10}$*

8 What is the **next number**? 4, 9, 14, 19, 24,   *29*

9 How many **right angles** are there in this figure?   *4*

10 The **sum** of 75 and 33 is   *100*

11 **Subtract** 59 from 78   *19*

12 What is the **product** of 63 and 10?   *73*

13 Round 45 to the **nearest** 10   *66*

14 Round 63 to the **nearest** 10   *60*

15 Round 18 cm to the **nearest 10 cm**   *20*

e.g. __3__ and __4__ are pair of **factors** of **12**. The **sum** of factors equals __7__

16-17 __2,3__ and ___5___ are pair of **factors** of **15**. The **sum** of the factors
equals ___8___

7

2

3

3

2

24

18-19 __2__ and __5__ are pair of **factors** of **10**. The **sum** of the factors equals __7__

Ring the answer.

20 12 - 2 + 10 = 24 (20) 0 18

21 29 + 1 + 30 = 30 31 (60) 61

22 4 x 1 x 10 = (40) 14 41 400

23 What is 9 **more than** 9 x 5 ? __54__

24 What is 6 **less than** 6 x 8 ? __42__

25 Which is an **even number** ? Tick (✓)

| 1 | 13 | 19 | 29 | (30) |

26 What is the **next number?**

| 981 | 882 | 783 | 684 | 585 |

27 In a row of students, Jim is **fifth** from either ends of the row.
How many students are there in the row? __9 students__

Tick (✓) what direction will you face, If you start facing

28 West and turn **one right angle** in clockwise

| East | South | North |

29 South and turn **three right angle** anti-clock wise

| (North) | West | East |

30 Write **ten minutes** to **eight** in the morning in figures using **am** or **pm.**

_____

Tick (✓) the correct one.

31 **Place value** of 9 in 8954 is

| 9 | 90 | (900) | 9000 |

32 **7.45** am on a 24-hour clock is

| (07:45) | 29:45 | 31:45 | 19:45 |

33 The **triangular number** shown in the pattern is

| 4 | | 8 | | 9 | | 10 |

34 Better **unit** to measure **volume** in a cup of milk

| *l* | | ml | | kg | | g |

35 Ten greater than **smallest** three digit number

| 100 | | 101 | | 110 | | 990 |

3

1

36 Write two thousand nine hundred and ten in **figure**. _____

Write the answer.

37 8 + 8 + 8 = ☐ 24 ☐ x 8   **38** 8 - 8 + 8 = ☐ 1 ☐ x 8

39 8 x 8 ÷ 8 = ☐ 8 ☐ x 8   **40** 80 ÷ 10 + 8 = ☐ 2 ☐ x 8

4

Know it

Multiply a number by 10.
Write that number and add a 0 on its right.

e.g. 5 x 10 = 50
    29 x 10 = 290

Multiply a number by 100.
Write that number and add a 00 on its right.

e.g. 19 x 100 = 1,900
    981 x 100 = 98,100

Multiply a number by 20, 30, 40....

Step 1 : Multiply the number by 2, 3, 4 ....

Step 2 : Add 0 on its right

e.g. 23 x 20 = 23 x 2 x 10 = 46 x 10 = 460
    29 x 30 = 29 x 3 x 10 = 87 x 10 = 870
    13 x 40 = 13 x 4 x 10 = 52 x 10 = 520

Three Dots Group

Count | **40** | %

Write the location in (X Y) form.

y₆					
y₅				POST BOX	
y₄	MALL				
y₃	ATM			HOUSE	
y₂		SCHOOL			
y₁					
	x₁	x₂	x₃	x₄	x₅	x₆

e.g. Where is the school? $(x_3\ y_2)$ **1** Where is the house ? ___ x_5, y_3

2 Where is the mall? ___ x_2, y_4 **3** Where is the post box ? x_5, y_5

4 Where is the ATM? ___ x_1, y_3 **5** Shade the box $(x_4\ y_1)$ **5**

Change the given number words in **figures.**

6 Two hundred and one _____ 301

7 One hundred and fifty six _____ 156

8 Four hundred and thirty two _____ 432

9 Sixty Two _____ 62

10 Nine hundred and ninety nine _____ 990   **5**

Find the time duration between

| 11 | 11 : 05 | and | 11 : 35 | _30_ minutes |
| 12 | 10 : 30 | and | 10 : 50 | _20_ minutes |

Write the number which is a **multiple** of 5.

13 24   31   36   40   42   _47_

14 35   42   49   56   59   _64_

Look at the figure.

15 A number in the **rectangle** and the **circle**. _30_

16 A number in the **square** and the **circle**. _5_

17 Which number is only in the **circle**? _35_

18 **Sum** of all numbers in the **rectangle** _75_

19 **Sum** of all numbers in the **square** _36_

20 **Sum** of all numbers in the **circle** _70_

21 **Sum** of all numbers in the **circle** and **square** _100_

22-28 Complete the table with **multiples** of 5 upto 51.

| Odd | 5 | 15 | 25 | 35 | 45 |
| Even | 10 | 20 | 30 | 40 | 50 |

29 How many **multiples** of 10 are there in the table? _12_

Look at the **rectangle.**

30 How many **squares** form 1/2 of the **rectangle**? _6_

Tick (✓) the correct one.

31 **Place value** of 2 in 2910 is

| 2 | 20 | 200 | 2000 |

32 2 hours in minutes equal to

| 60 | (120) | 50 | 100 |

33   **Product** of 10 and x is written as

| $x\ 10$ | $x + 10$ | $x - 10$ | $10\ x$ |

(10 x circled)

34   Number of days in 4 weeks

| 21 | 28 | 24 | 32 |

(28 circled)

35   Number of **zeros** in ten thousand

| 4 | 3 | 5 | 6 |

(4 circled)

36   Write **10 minutes after nine** in the morning in figure using **am** or **pm**.

$\underline{9{:}10\ am}$

Write the answer.

37   5 + 0 = $\boxed{5}$

38   0 ÷ 5 = $\boxed{0}$

39   5 - 0 = $\boxed{5}$

40   0 x 5 = $\boxed{0}$

3

1

4

Know it

Multiply a number by 200, 300, 400....

Step 1 : Multiply the number by 2, 3, 4 ....

Step 2 : Add 00 on its right

e.g.   16 x 200 = 16 x 2 x 100 =   32 x 100 =   3,200

27 x 300 = 27 x 3 x 100 =   81 x 100 =   8,100

62 x 400 = 62 x 4 x 100 = 248 x 100 =   24,800

Multiply a number with the sum of two other numbers.

e.g.   4 x (3 + 2)

Method 1 :   4 x (3 + 2) = 4 x 3 + 4 x 2 = 12 + 18 = 20

Method 2 :   4 x (3 + 2) = 4 x 5 = 20

Multiply a number with the difference of two other numbers.

e.g.   5 x (12 - 4)

Method 1 :   5 x (12 - 4) = 5 x 12 - 5 x 4 = 60 - 20 = 40

Method 2 :   5 x (12 - 4) = 5 x 8 = 40

Three Dots Group

Count | **40** | %

The bar chart shows the type of sports people like.

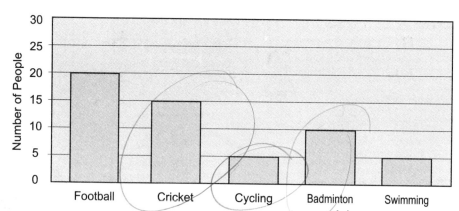

1   Which is the **most** popular sport? _Foot Ball_

2   How many people like cricket? _15_

3   _5_ [**more**] people like cricket than badminton.

4   Same number of people like swimming and _Cycling_ .

5   10 **less** people prefer badminton than _Foot Ball_ .

6   **Total** number of people who like cycling and _____ is 20.

Write the answer from the expression **A** and **B**.

| A | □ + □ + □ + □ = 20 |
| B | △ - □ = 10 |

□ = 5
△ =

7   □ = _5_   8   △ = _15_

9   □ + □ = _10_   10   △ + △ = _30_

11   □ + △ = _20_   12   △ + △ - □ = _25_

6

6

Put the correct sign **<** or **>** in the space.

e.g. 5 **<** 7 means 5 **less** than 7 and 9 **>** 4 means 9 **greater** than 4

13   13 ____ 31   14   83 ____ 54

15   9 ____ (20 ÷ 2)   16   16 ____ (5 x 3)

17   (4 x 3) ____ (5 x 2) 18   (100 ÷ 2) ____ (20 x 3)   **6**

Find the pair of numbers when the **sum** and **product** are given.

	Sum	Product	Pair of numbers		
e.g.	7	6	__1__	and	__6__
19-20	19	18	__1__	and	__18__
21-22	13	42	__1__	and	__42__
23-24	17	60	__1__	and	__60__
25-26	21	110	__1__	and	__110__

8

27   I have 6 faces, all the faces are squares of same size. I am a ___?___ .

Tick (✓) in the box.

☐ cone   ☐ sphere   ☑ cube   ☐ cuboid   **1**

Write the answer using the table.

Item	Cost
Chips	20p
Pizza	80p
Cream bun	40p

28   Jack bought 2 packets of chips and 1 pizza. How much he has to pay? ___£1.20___

29   Jill gave **£ 2** to buy 3 cream buns and 1 packet of chips. How much did he get back? ___40p Back___

30   For buying 2 pizzas and 2 cream buns, Alan should pay exactly ___£2.40___   **3**

Cross **(x)** the odd one.

31 | pen | | pencil | | chalk | | ~~spoon~~ |

32 | 101 | | (405) | | 303 | | 202 |

33   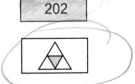   **3**

31

A group photograph shows 13 men standing in a row. Mr. Pole is in the centre.

34 What is Pole's position from the left? _____

35 What is Pole's position from the right? _____

36 What is **6 pm** on a 24-hour clock? _____18.00_____

18.00

Write the answer.

37 11 + 1 = [12]

38 11 x 1 = [11]

39 11 - 1 = [10]

40 11 ÷ 1 = [11]

2

1

4

Know it

Note:

- Adding two or more numbers in any order, their sum will remain the same.
  e.g. 62 + 83 = 83 + 62 = 145

- Any number added to zero, the sum is the number itself.
  e.g. 19 + 0 = 0 + 19 = 19

- Any number added to its negative, the sum is zero.
  e.g. -16 + 16 = 16 + (-16) = 0

- When 0 is subtracted from any number, the result is the number itself.
  e.g.1 29 - 0 = 29   **e.g.2** 30 - 0 = 30

- Two numbers can be multiplied in any order.
  e.g. 6 x 5 = 5 x 6 = 30

DIVISION

Repeated subtraction method.

e.g.1 Divide 36 by 12

36 - Dividend
12 - Divisor or Divider

```
  36
-  12   ← First
  24
-  12   ← Second
  12
-  12   ← Third
   0    Remainder 0, Quotient 3
```

36 ÷ 12 = 3

number of subtraction is **Quotient.**

e.g.2 Divide 19 by 6

19 - Dividend
6 - Divisor or Divider

```
  19
-  6    ← First
  13
-  6    ← Second
   7
-  6    ← Third
   1    Remainder 1, Quotient 3
```

19 ÷ 6 = 3, remainder 1

Three Dots Group

Count [**40**] [**%**]

The graph shows wake up time of Class III students on Sunday.

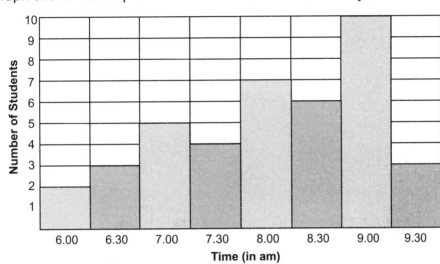

1   At what time do **least** students wake up? ___6:00___

2   How many students wake up at **7.00 am**? ___5___

3   At what time do **most** students wake up? ___9:00___

4   How many students wake up from **7.00 am** to **8.00 am**? ___17___

5   How many students in class III? ___40___

5

Look at the Venn diagram.

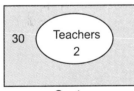

6   How many gents are teachers? ___2___

7   How many ladies are teachers? ___10___

8   How many ladies who are not teachers? ___35___

9   How many gents who are not teachers? ___30___

10 Altogether, How many teachers? ___12___

5

⟨33⟩

Write the **missing term.**

11	3	_6_	9	12	15	18
12	20	30	40	50	60	_70_
13	80	75	70	_65_	60	55
14	_12_	16	20	24	28	32

Write the answers.

15
£ 2 . 46
+ £ 5 . 32
_£7.78_

16
£ 4 . 07
+ £ 2 . 14
_£6 21_

17
£ 3 . 21
+ £ 1 . 23
_£4.44_

18
£ 4 . 09
+ £ 2 . 06
_£6.05_

19 How many shaded portions make 6?

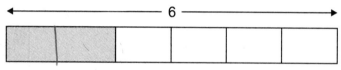

_2/6_

Write the **fraction** of shaded part in the lowest term.

20 ⊕ = _1/4_

21  = _1/2 or 3/6_

22 ⊕ = _3/4_

23 = _1/2 or 6/12_

24 ☆☆☆☆☆☆ = _2/6_

25-26 Write 79 and 87 in the **number track.**

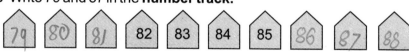

79 80 81 82 83 84 85 86 87 88

27-28 Write 10 and 55 in the **number track.**

10 15 20 25 30 35 40 45 50 55

29-30 Write 104 and 120 in the **number track**.

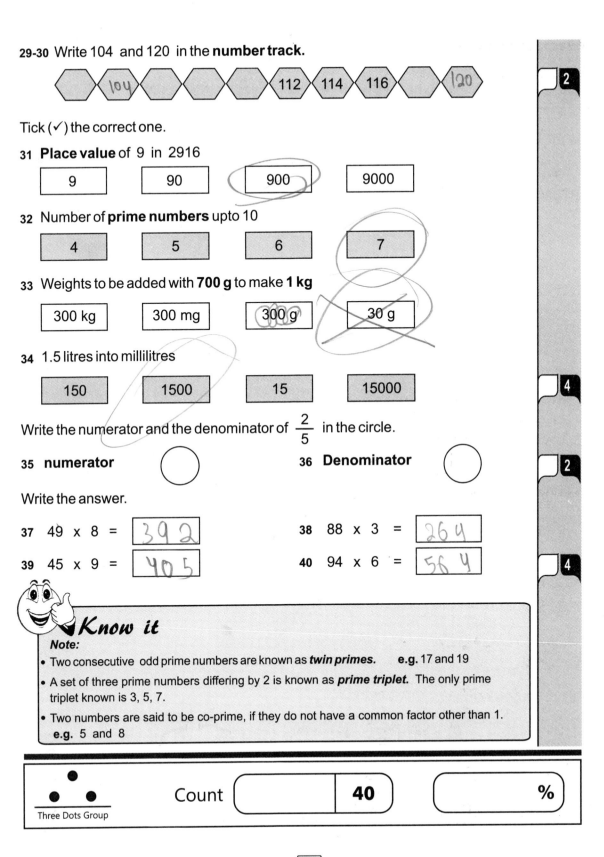

| | 104 | | | | 112 | 114 | 116 | | 120 | | **2** |

Tick (✓) the correct one.

31 **Place value** of 9 in 2916

| 9 | 90 | (900) | 9000 |

32 Number of **prime numbers** upto 10

| 4 | 5 | 6 | 7 |

33 Weights to be added with **700 g** to make **1 kg**

| 300 kg | 300 mg | 300 g | 30 g |

34 1.5 litres into millilitres

| 150 | 1500 | 15 | 15000 | | **4** |

Write the numerator and the denominator of $\dfrac{2}{5}$ in the circle.

35 **numerator** ◯   **36** **Denominator** ◯   **2**

Write the answer.

37 49 x 8 = 392   **38** 88 x 3 = 264

39 45 x 9 = 405   **40** 94 x 6 = 564   **4**

Know it

Note:

- Two consecutive odd prime numbers are known as *twin primes.*   **e.g.** 17 and 19
- A set of three prime numbers differing by 2 is known as *prime triplet.* The only prime triplet known is 3, 5, 7.
- Two numbers are said to be co-prime, if they do not have a common factor other than 1.
  e.g. 5 and 8

Three Dots Group

Count | 40 | %

Use the pictograph of Class III students and write the answers.

Favourite TV channels	Each ☐ stands for 2 students
Sports	☐ ☐ ☐
Cartoon	☐ ☐ ☐ ☐ ☐
Comedy	☐ ☐ ☐ ☐
Adventure	☐ ☐

1 How many students like adventure channel? _____ 4

2 Which is the **most** popular channel? _____ cartoon

3 How many students like sports channel? _____ 6 people

4 How many **more** students like comedy than sports? _____ 2

5 How many students like cartoon channel? _____ 10

6 **Total** number of students in class III is _____ 28   **6**

Put the sign < or > or = in the space.

7 comedy ___>___ sports

8 adventure ___<___ cartoon

9 sports and comedy ___=___ cartoon and adventure   **3**

Write the answer in the space also fill in **O** for **odd** number and **E** for **even** number

for the answer in the box.

10-11 2 + 2 = ___4___ is [E] number

12-13 5 + 3 = ___8___ is [E] number

14-15 7 + 4 = ___11___ is [O] number

16-17 8 + 9 = ___17___ is [O] number   **8**

18-23 Write the given numbers in the **Venn diagram.**

U - numbers   A - multiple of 4

8   12   10   16   20   24

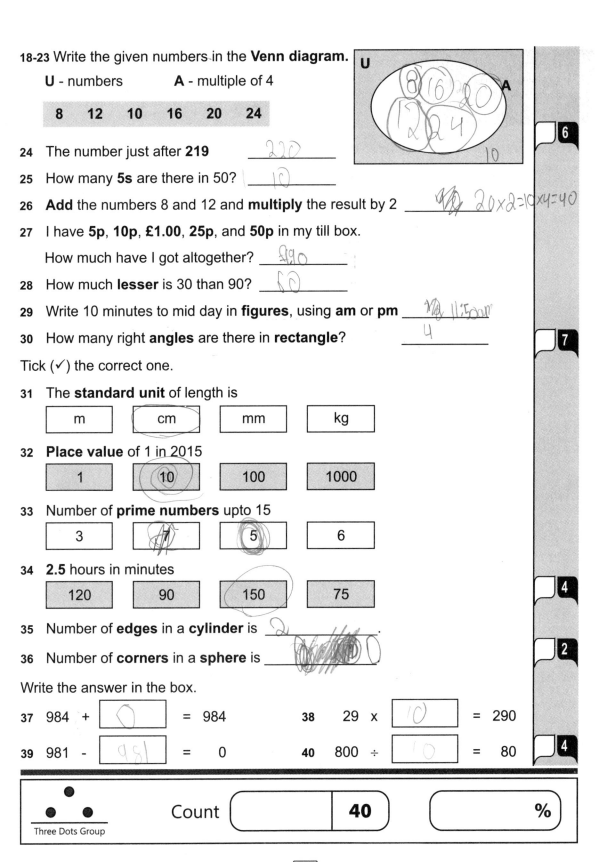

24 The number just after **219**   220

25 How many **5s** are there in 50?   10

26 **Add** the numbers 8 and 12 and **multiply** the result by 2   20×2=10×4=40

27 I have **5p**, **10p**, **£1.00**, **25p**, and **50p** in my till box.

How much have I got altogether?   £190

28 How much **lesser** is 30 than 90?   60

29 Write 10 minutes to mid day in **figures**, using **am** or **pm**   11:50am

30 How many right **angles** are there in **rectangle**?   4

Tick (✓) the correct one.

31 The **standard unit** of length is

| m | cm | mm | kg |

32 **Place value** of 1 in 2015

| 1 | 10 | 100 | 1000 |

33 Number of **prime numbers** upto 15

| 3 | 7 | 5 | 6 |

34 **2.5** hours in minutes

| 120 | 90 | 150 | 75 |

35 Number of **edges** in a **cylinder** is _____

36 Number of **corners** in a **sphere** is _____

Write the answer in the box.

37 984 + 0 = 984

38 29 x 10 = 290

39 981 - 981 = 0

40 800 ÷ 10 = 80

6

7

4

2

4

Count   **40**   %

Three Dots Group

37

Venn diagram shows the favourite food of 12 children from **a** to *l*.

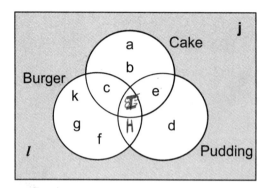

1   Who like only cake?   _____ ~~j~~ a b

2   Which is the most favourite food?   _____ Burger

3   Who like cake and burgar?   _____ H

4   Who like all the three?   _____ I

5-8 Who like pudding?   _____ d

9   Who like cake and pudding?   _____ e

10-11 Who unlike all the three?   _____ j 6 or l

11

Write the **fraction** of shaded part.

12   _____ $\frac{1}{2}$ **one - half**

13   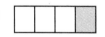   _____ $\frac{1}{4}$ **one-fourth**

14   _____ $\frac{2}{3}$ **two-thirds**

15-16      _____ $\frac{1}{3}$ one-third

5

Count the dots and fill the table.

#	Dots	Equation
17	(• •)	2 x 1 = 2
18	(• •) (• •)	2 x 2 = 4
19-20	(• •) (• •) (• •)	2 x 3 = 6
21	dice(3) dice(3)	3 x 2 = 6
22-23	dice(3) dice(3) dice(3)	3 x 3 = 9
24-26	dice(4) dice(4) dice(4) dice(3)	3 x 4 = 12

27 If you **multiply** the number 10 by 5 and **add** 7, what is the number you get?
_____ 57 _____

28 When you **multiply** a number by 10 and **add** 3, you get 73. What is the number? _____ 7 _____

Draw the possible **lines of symmetry.**

29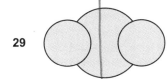

30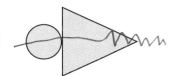

Cross (**x**) the odd one out.

31 | 2 | 5 | 7 | 14 |

32 | $\frac{A}{1}$ | $\frac{B}{2}$ | $\frac{C}{6}$ | $\frac{D}{4}$ |

33 | Square | Circle | Triangle | Rectangle |

34

35 What is double the difference between 16 and 29 ? _____ 26 _____

26

〈39〉

36 What fraction of a day is 18 hours? $\frac{18}{24}$ or $\frac{9}{12}$

Write the answer.

37 60 + 30 = `90`   **38** 60 - 30 = `30`

39 35 + 15 = `50`   **40** 35 - 15 = `10`

Know it

Short Division Method

e.g. Divide 981 by 4

$$4\overline{\smash)9\,{}^18\,{}^21} \quad \begin{array}{ccc}2 & 4 & 5\end{array} \quad \text{Rem 1}$$

Quotient →	2 4 5	Rem 1 ← Remainder
Divisor → 4	9 8 1	← Dividend

9 ÷ 4 = 2, Rem. 1
Write 2 and carry the 1, you get 18
18 ÷ 4 = 4, Rem. 2
Write 4 and carry the 2, you get 21
21 ÷ 4 = 5, Rem.1
Write 5 and the remainder 1

Use this method when **dividing** by a single digit.

Long Division Method

e.g. Divide 30 by 7

```
      4  ←
  7 ) 30
    - 28   ← 7x4
    ------
      2
```

Multiple of 7 must be **less than** and very close to 30

Rough Work
7 x 2 = 14
7 x 3 = 21
7 x 4 = 28
7 x 5 = 35

Dividend   - 30
Divisor   - 7
Quotient   - 4
Remainder   - 2

Dividend = Divisor x Quotient + Remainder
   30   =   7   x   4   +   2

Count **40**   %

Look at the chart.

1-10 Write the answer and its code letter in the box.

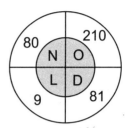

1 x 9	30 x 7	16 x 5	9 x 9	7 x 30	5 x 16
9	210	**80**	81	210	80
L	O	**N**	D	O	N

11 What was the city? _LONDON_

12 What **fraction** of an hour is 10 minutes? _10/60_ _1/6_

13 **Doubling** a number gives the same result as **adding** 10 and 8.
What is the number? _9 doubled_

Look at the letters.   R S V X Z

14 Which letter has one **line of symmetry**? _V_

15 Which letter has two **lines of symmetry**? _X_

Each shape represent a digit. Find the result **R**.

♡ = 2   ♠ = 5   ◇ = 8   ♣ = 10

16 R = ♡ + ♡
R = _4_

17 R = ♡ + ◇
R = _10_

18 R = ♠ - ♡
R = _3_

19 R = ♣ ÷ ♠
R = _2_

20 R = ♡ x ◇
R = _16_

21 R = ♡ + ◇ + ◇
R = _18_

11

2

2

6

22 R = ♡² + ♠⁵ + ◇⁸ + ♣¹⁰

R = ___25___ .

23 11 children are in a queue and the distance between two of them is **50 cm**.

How long is the queue? ___550 cm___

Build the **smallest** and the **greatest** 3-digit number.

	Digits	Smallest number	Greatest number
24-25	5, 4, 7	457	754
26-27	0, 6, 9	609	960

28 The **product** of two numbers is 40. One number is 5.

The other number is ___35___ .

29 Cost of 2 burgers **£ 1.00**, then the cost of 6 burgers ___£3·00___ .

Tick (✓) the correct answer.

30 Which is the **largest**?

| 2 m 4 cm | | 240 cm | | (680 cm) | | 6 m 8 cm |

31 The number between 994 and 984

| 994 | | (984) | | 989 | | (980) |

32 **Perimeter** of a **square** with a side of 2 cm is

| 4 cm | | 6 cm | | (8 cm) | | 2 cm |

33 Number of weeks in 21 days

| (3) | | 1 | | 2 | | 4 |

34 (3 : 9) (5 : 15) (7 : 21) (? : 30)

| 2 | | 7 | | 10 | | (8) |

1

1

4

2

5

Write the **smallest** and **greatest** three-digit number using the digits 5, 0 and 2

35 **Smallest** | 2 | 0 | 5 | **36** **Greatest** | 5 | 2 | 0 |

Write the answer.

37 7 x 1 = | 7 |

38 1 x 9 = | 9 |

39 6 x 0 = | 0 |

40 0 x 8 = | 0 |

Know it

e.g.2 Divide 6284 by 13

```
              483   Quotient
Divisor 13 ⟌ 6284
          -52↓     ← 13x4
          ─────
           108
          -104↓    ←- 13x8
          ─────
            44
           -39     ← 13x3
          ─────
             5     Remainder
```

6 less than 13, cannot be divided by 13

Rough Work
13 x 1 = 13
13 x 2 = 26
13 x 3 = 39
13 x 4 = 52
13 x 5 = 65
13 x 6 = 78
13 x 7 = 91
13 x 8 = 104
13 x 9 = 117

62 ÷ 13   ⇒   62 = **4** x 13 + 10 = 52 + 10
write 4 in the answer, 10 left over
Bring down 8, you get 108

108 ÷ 13   ⇒   108 = **8** x 13 + 4 = 104 + 4
write 8 in the answer, 4 left over
Bring down 4, you get 44

44 ÷ 13   ⇒   44 = **3** x 13 + 5 = 39 + 5
write 3 in the answer, 5 left over
The remainder is 5.

Note:
- Divide any number (except 0) by itself, the quotient is 1.
  e.g.1   5 ÷ 5 = 1   **e.g.2**   16 ÷ 16 = 1

Three Dots Group

Count | **40** |

%

Unscramble the words and match their shapes:

1-2   R C E I C L   *circle*

3-4   C N O E   *cone*

5-6   D O C U I B   *cuboid*

e.g. S A R U Q E   SQUARE

7-8   P S H R E E   *sphere*

9   Galis has **£5.00** while Craig has **£2.00** more than him. How much do they have altogether?   *12*

Tick (✓) the answer.

10   **Length** of the bat is about

| 1 cm | 10 cm | (1 m) | 10 m |

11   Spoon can hold about

| 50 ml | 50 *l* | 5 *l* | (5 ml) |

12   Write 84 to the **nearest** 10   *80*

13   Write 97 to the **nearest** 10   *100*

14   Write 386 to the **nearest** 100   *400*

Draw the **mirror lines** on the shape.

15   **16**   **17**   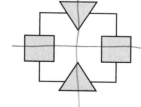

Write the answer.

18   40 x 10 = 4   x 100   = __400__

19-20 70 x 10 = 7   x 100   = __700__

21   60 ÷ 10 = 6   x   10   ÷ 10   = __6__

22-23 900 ÷ 10 = 90   x 10 ÷ 10   = __90__

24-25 Write the next two numbers in the **sequence.**

   12   16   20   24   __28__   __32__

26   Write five hundred and seventy six in **figures** __576__

27   Write the number.

   1 **hundred** 6 **tens** 5 **units** = __165__

Write the expanded form.

28   257 = __2__ **hundred** __5__ **tens** __7__ **units**

29   257 = __200__   +   __50__   +   __7__

30   Use the digits **9, 0, 7** and write the **smallest** three-digit number __709__

Tick (✓) the correct one.

31 Smallest 4-digit number using the digits **2, 0, 6** and **1**

| 2016 | 6210 | 2061 | 1026 |

32 Volume of an average human stomach is **1*l*,** then $\frac{1}{5}$ of the volume is

| 20 *l* | 40 *l* | 400 ml | 200 ml |

33 Area of a square having side of **5 cm** is

| 25 cm | 40 cm | 40 cm^2 | 25 cm^2 |

34 The **rectangular** number is

| 5 | 7 | 13 | 15 |

35 Decrease **two thousand** by **six hundred** in figures __1400__

36 Round 49 to the **nearest ten** __50__

Write the missing number in the box.

37 5 = $\dfrac{\boxed{5}}{10}$

38 7 = $\dfrac{21}{\boxed{7}}$

39 1 = $\dfrac{\boxed{1}}{5}$

40 1 = $\dfrac{10}{\boxed{1}}$

Know it

- Divide any number by 1, the quotient is the number itself.
  e.g.1 $4 \div 1 = 4$ **e.g.2** $19 \div 1 = 19$

- Divide 0 by any number (except 0) the quotient is 0.
  e.g.1 $0 \div 2 = 0$ **e.g.2** $0 \div 30 = 0$

- Divide any number by 0 never comes to an end. So we cannot divide a number by 0.

Inverse Operations

The word Inverse Operation is known as opposite operation that undo each other.

- Addition ⟷ Subtraction
  + sign   and   - sign   are Inverse

- Multiple ⟷ Division
  x sign   and   ÷ sign   are Inverse

It can be explained simply by a triangle

Operation of any two vertices = Third vertex

e.g.1 $3 + 5 = 8$
$8 - 3 = 5$
$8 - 5 = 3$

e.g.2 $3 \times 2 = 6$
$6 \div 2 = 3$
$6 \div 3 = 2$

- Also square and square root are Inverse operations.

  Square ⟷ Square Root
  $(\ \ )^2$ $\sqrt{\ \ }$

5^2

5   25

$\sqrt{25}$

Three Dots Group

Count | **40** | %

46

A   B   C

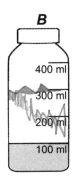 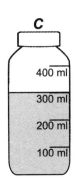

A	B	C
400 ml	400 ml	400 ml
300 ml	300 ml	300 ml
200 ml	200 ml	200 ml
100 ml	100 ml	100 ml

Volume of water is shown in each bottle.

1   What is the **volume** of water in **A** ?   _220_ ml

2   Which has the **highest volume**?   _C_

3   What is the **total volume** of water in **A** and **B** ?   _340_ ml

4   What is the **difference** in volume of **A** and **C** ?   _100_ ml

5   Write the **fraction** of water in **A**.   _220/400_

6   **Total volume** of water in **A, B** and **C**   _660_ ml

7   If 50% of water from **A** is poured into **B**, the new volume of **B** is _230_ ml

8   What is the **maximum** capacity of all three bottles?   _400_ ml   **8**

_or 1200_

Write the answer using **am** or **pm**.

9   10 minutes past 7 in the morning is _7:10 am_

10 Quarter past 6 in the morning is _6:20 am_

11 What is the **product** of 5 and 3 ? _8_   **3**

12-13 Write the next two numbers.

   15   30   45   _60_   _75_   **2**

Write the answer.

14-15 3 **tens** 9 **units** = _3/ten_ = _3 units_ x 3   **2**

16-17 4 **tens** ____ **units** = 46 = 23 x ____

18 44 + 44 + 44 + 44 = __4__ x 44

Change the **sign** to correct the **equation.**

19 5 + 3 = 2

5 [—] 3 = 2

20 20 ÷ 5 = 100

20 [X] 5 = 100

21 15 - 5 = 3

15 [÷] 5 = 3

22 5 + 5 + 5 = 5

5 + 5 [−] 5 = 5

23 10 x 2 + 5 = 10

10 [÷] 2 + 5 = 10

24 10 + 10 + 10 = 3 + 10

10 + 10 + 10 = 3 [X] 10

25 **Fraction** of squares being crossed

$\dfrac{2}{5}$

26 The three-digit number end as _____

27 Cost of one cake slice is 20p. Find the cost 6 slices of cake £ _____

Draw the **lines of symmetry.**

28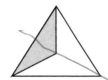

29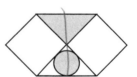

30 A painter is engaged to write serial numbers from 1 to 15. How many times will he be required to write 1 ? _____

Tick (✓) the correct one.

31 **Greatest** 4-digit number using the digits 9, 1, 0 and 2

| 2910 | 2109 | 2019 | (9210) |

32 One cup of milk can be **equal** to

| 2 g | (20 g) | 200 g | 2 kg |

3

6

1

2

2

1

2

33 The letter having one **line of symmetry** is

| G | H | P | M |

34 Weights to be added on **600 g** to make **1 kg**

| 4 kg | 400 g | 40 g | 400 mg |

35 A number gets **doubled** if its increased by 15. What is the number?

15

36 Kicky is **20 years** old. Her father is 3 times as old as Kicky. How old is he?

60

2

Write the answer.

37 6^2 = 36

38 $6^2 - 5^2$ = 41

39 9^2 = 81

40 $9^2 - 8^2$ = 17

4

Know it

- A number multiplied by itself is a square number.

  e.g. $5^2 = 5 \times 5 = 25$

- A square root of a number is a value when multiplied by itself gives the original number.

  e.g. $\sqrt{25} = \sqrt{5 \times 5} = 5$

Divisibility of a number

- **A number is divisible by 2**, if it has any of the digits 0, 2, 4, 6 or 8 in its units place.

  e.g. 30, 62, 84, 16, 178 ... are divisible by 2.

- **A number is divisible by 3**, if the sum of its digits is divisible by 3.

  e.g. 91983 is divisible by 3, since sum of its digits 9 + 1 + 9 + 8 + 3 = 30 is divisible by 3.

- **A number is divisible by 4**, if the last two digits of it is divisible by 4.

  e.g. 1984 is divisible by 4, since 84 is divisible by 4.

Three Dots Group

Count 40

%

Write the missing numbers in the table.

1-4

Multiples of 5	5	10	15	20	25	30	35	40

4

5-12 Fill all the numbers from the table in **Venn diagram.**

U - multiples of 5

A - even numbers

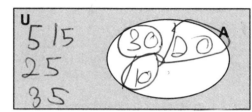

8

13 How many **odd** numbers are there in Venn diagram? _O_

14 How many **multiples** of 20 are there in Venn diagram? _O_

15 How many **multiples** of 15 are there in Venn diagram? _O_

3

Balance the **equation.**

16 4 x 5 = 12 + _8_   **17** 7 x _3_ = 19 + 2

2

18 How many 20p will make **£1.00**? _~~4~~ 5_

19 Tim poured **200 ml** milk in the jug, What fraction of milk is in the jug? $\frac{2}{5}$

20 Write two hundred and five in **figures.** _205_

21 My watch is 2 minutes a head. It shows **08:17.**
What is the correct time? _08:15_

22 Write 10 minutes to ten at night in **figures**, using **am** or **pm** _9:50pm_ ~~_____~~

5

23 Write the fraction in order beginning with the **smallest.**

$\frac{1}{2}$, $\frac{3}{4}$, $\frac{1}{4}$ $\frac{3}{5}$, $\frac{1}{4}$, $\frac{1}{2}$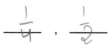

1

24 The **sum** of 10, 12 and 20 is _42_

1

Shade the **last** circle to balance the **equation.**

25   $\dfrac{1}{4}$ + $\dfrac{1}{4}$ = $\dfrac{1}{2}$

   +   =

26   $\dfrac{3}{4}$ + $\dfrac{1}{4}$ =   1

   +   =

27   $\dfrac{3}{4}$ - $\dfrac{1}{4}$ = $\dfrac{1}{2}$

   -      = 

28   Catch out my date of birth, two tens and a nine   _29 1019_

29   Catch out my date of birth, four fours and a three   _4443_

30   Halfway number between 8 and 24 is   _19443 16_

Tick (✓) the correct one.

31   **Divide** the **greatest** number of 3-digit by 3

| 999 | 993 | 111 | (333) |

32   The number that is exactly **divisible** by 5

| 12 | (10) | 16 | 36 |

33   A two-digit **prime number** less than 20, whose **units** digit is 3

| (13) | 11 | 23 | 43 |

34   **Perimeter** of a **rectangle** with sides 4 cm and 2 cm is

| 6 cm | 8 cm | 12 cm | (18 cm) |

35   The number which is a **factor** of every number is _____

36 3 hours before **1pm** is ___10:00 am___

Write the answer.

37 49 + 19 = 68

38 52 - 12 = 40

39 29 + 31 = 60

40 67 - 17 = 50

Know it

- **A number is divisible by 5**, if it has either 0 or 5 in its units place.

  e.g. 20, 850, 65, 275 ..... are divisible by 5.

- **A number is divisible by 6**, if the number is divisible by 2 and 3.

  e.g. 61962 is divisible by 6, since it is divisible by 2 and 3.

- **A number is divisible by 7**, if you take the last digit, double it, subtract it from the remaining number and the result is divisible by 7.

  e.g. 1715 divisibly by   7   since,

  the last digit is   5

  double of 5 is   10

  subtract 10 from 171 which is 161 divisible by 7.

- **A number is divisible by 8**, if the last three digits of it is divisible by 8.

  e.g. 30168 is divisible by 8, since 168 is divisible by 8.

- **A number is divisible by 9**, if the sum of its digits is divisible by 9.

  e.g. 190116 is divisible by 9, since sum of its digits 1+9+0+1+1+6 = 18 is divisible by 9.

- **A number is divisible by 10**, if it has 0 in its units place.

  e.g. 30, 19,830, 296,620.... are divisible by 10.

- A number divisible by co-prime number is divisible by their product.

  e.g. 80 is divisible by 4 and 5.

  80 is also divisible by 20 since 4 x 5 = 20.

- If there is no remainder, the quotient and divisor are the **factors** of the dividend.

- If there is no remainder, the dividend is a **multiple** of the quotient and divisor.

Harry stands in the centre facing North.

J - Jame's house
C - Church
L - Louise's house
M - Mall

N - North
E - East
S - South
W - West

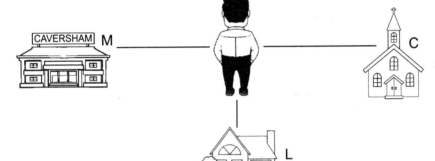

1   Church is _____East_____ of mall.

2   Mall is _____west_____ of Harry.

3   If Harry made a right turn, then he will face _____Church_____

4   Harry faces North and made a left turn, he will now face _____Mall_____

5   Louise's house is _____South_____ of Jame's house.

6   Harry turns from **N** to **E**, then he is facing _____church_____

7   Harry turns **N** to **S**, then he is facing _____L_____

8   Harry faces **N** and made half right angle turn clockwise. What direction is he now facing? _____church_____

9   Harry faces **S** and made three right angle turns clockwise. What direction is he now facing? _____East_____   **9**

10 A maths class started at **5.30 pm** and ended at **6.40 pm**. How long was the class? _____70_____ min

11 My watch is 10 minutes fast. It shows **20 minutes past 3**, then the right time is _____3:10_____   **2**

12 The **difference** between the **place value** and **face value** of 8 in

1 9 8 3 is _____ .

13 How many **odd** numbers are from 1 to 5? _____3_____

14 How many **even** numbers between 16 and 30? _____2_____

15 What is the greatest number of pens can be bought for **£ 1.00** ?

 each **7p**    3 for **20p**   15

16 Andy has a ribbon of length **80 cm**. She cut it into 5 equal pieces.
How long is each piece? _____15_____ .

Look at the exchange rate.

£ 1.00	=	$ 1.62
$ 1.00	=	£ 0.62

17 Anne wants **£100** in US dollars, how much will she get? $ _____

18 A shirt costs **$100**, how much is this in pound sterling?   £ _____

19 A burger costs **$10** is equivalent to   £ _____

20 Raisin cake costs **£10** is equivalent to $ _____

Measure the length by using a ruler.

21    _____ cm

22   _____ cm

Find the numbers **a** and **b**.

Sum	Product	a	and	b
23 a + b = 5	a x b = 6	2	and	3
24 a + b = 10	a x b = 21	3	and	7
25 a + b = 8	a x b = 15	3	and	5
26 a + b = 26	a x b = 25	___	and	___

27 How many squares you need to form a cube?   _____

28 I am a two-digit number and **multiple** of 10. I have six in ten's place. What number am I? _____ 60

Draw the **lines** of **symmetry.**

29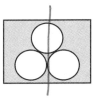

30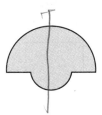

Cross (x) the odd one out.

31 Expected **temperature** in a bowl of soup is

| 120°c | 65°c | 70°c | 75°c |

32 Mary used **1 cup** of milk to make a pudding. The closest amount is

| 300 ml | 200 ml | 250 ml | 320 cm |

33 | 32 | 76 | 56 | 98 |

34

35 represents _____ 8

36 Numbers with **units** digit 5 or 0 are always **divisible** by _____ 50

Write the answer.

37 38 + 42 = | 80 |

38 $3^2 = 3 \times 3 =$ | 9 |

39 57 + 33 = | 90 |

40 $7^2 = 7 \times 7 =$ | 49 |

| Count | **40** | % |

Three Dots Group

Fill in the space with letters **A** to **H**.

 A   B   C   D

 E   F   G   H

1 Square	_B_	
3 Cylinder	_E_	
5 Hexagon	_G_	
7 Circle	_C_	

2 Sphere	_F F_	
4 Triangle	_A_	
6 Cone	_B_	
8 Pentagon	_H_	

9 Which shapes have only **curved** face?   _F C_

10 Which shapes have 3 **vertices**?   _A_

Which shapes have **plane** and **curved surface**?

11-12 _____ _D_ _____

13 Decrease five hundred by 100   _400_

14 Increase two hundred and fifty by 50   _300_

15 There are 12 pens in one box. How many pens are there in half a box?

_____

16 It takes mother 34 minutes to cook, which is **nearest 10 min** _____

17 My weight measures 39 kg, which is **nearest 10 kg** _____

18   £ 2. 25
   + £ 2. 75
   _____
   _____

19   £ 0. 35
   + £ 6. 21
   _____
   _____

20 The number which is 5 more than 19 is   _____

21 _____ is an **even number,** which comes just before 200.

22 A number **multiple** of 25 that follows 175   _____

8

4

5

2

3

23 Paul added eight hundred and six hundred, which in **figures** _____

24 I drink 200 ml milk each day. How long a 1 litre milk packet will last? _____ days

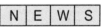

Tim is on the way to the park from his house. He crossed 200 m East, 100 m North, 200 m West and 300 m North. Where is the park from his house?

25 Shortest distance _____ m   **26** Tick (✓) the direction | N | E | W | S |

Look at the number machine. It follows the same rule each time when I put in a number.

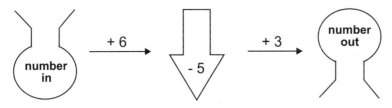

27 I put the number **20** into the machine. What number will come out?

_____

28 A number **34** comes out from the machine, then the number put into the machine is _____

29 My watch shows **3.00** and the minute hand points **North (N)**, then the hour hand points _____

30 What is the total number of legs in a group of 10 cows and 15 hens?

_____

Tick (✓) the correct one.

31 $\frac{1}{4}$ + $\frac{1}{4}$ is

| $\frac{1}{8}$ | | $\frac{1}{16}$ | | $\frac{2}{8}$ | | $\frac{1}{2}$ |

32 卌 卌 ||| represents

| 11 | | 12 | | 13 | | 5 |

57

33 An angle whose measure is between 0^0 and 90^0 is

Straight angle	Right angle	Acute angle	Obtuse angle

34

A A B : C	D D E : F	T T U : V	H H I : ?

F	G	J	K

35 Anderson is tenth from the left and seventh from the right in a line. How many people are there in the line?

14	40	17	16

3

36 5 years ago Tim was 10 years. His present age is _____ years.

1

Write the answer.

37 $\frac{1}{5}$ of 10 = [   ]   **38** $\frac{2}{3}$ of 9 = [   ]

39 $\frac{1}{10}$ of 40 = [   ]   **40** $\frac{3}{7}$ of 21 = [   ]

4

 Know it

Divide a number by 10

- If a number has 0 in the last digit, remove a 0. The number formed by the remaining digits is the quotient.

  e.g. $30 \div 10 = 3$ $290 \div 10 = 29$ $1600 \div 10 = 160$

  Q = 3, R = 0   Q = 29, R = 0   Q = 160, R = 0

- If a number has non - 0 in the last digit, take the last digit from the number as remainder. The number formed by the remaining digits is the quotient.

  e.g. $19 \div 10$ $983 \div 10$

  Remove 9 as remainder   Remove 3 as remainder

  leftover 1 as quotient   leftover 98 as quotient

  Q = 1, R = 9   Q = 98, R = 3

Three Dots Group

Count [| **40**]   [| **%**]

✓ Answers

1. 6
2. 6
3. 0 or no
4. 0 or no
5. △
6. ↑
7. 296
8. 271
9. 70
10. 80
11. 80
12. 20
13. Thursday
14. Friday
15. 8
16. Monday
17. 18
18. 8
19. 26
20. 126
21. even
22. 29
23. 44
24. 0
25. 50
26. M
27. V
28. 1000
29. 1
30. 2000
31. 2
32. 6
33. 3
34. 20
35. 1
36. 36
37. 5
38. 90
39. 4
40. 918

1. C
2. P
3. 4
4. B and V
5. 8
6. 11
7. 35
8. 200 m
9. 150 m
10. 350 m
11. Pin
12. 60
13. 70
14. 90
15. 300
16. 200
17. 5
18. 105
19. 240
20. 40
21. 50
22. 19
23. 24
24. 7
25. 9 m
26. 180

27. 12
28. 215
29. 7.15 am
30. 5.45 pm
31. 15
32. 21
33. ring
34. 953
35. 359
36. Class
37. 89
38. 40
39. 50
40. 10

1-3. (16) 8 D
4-6. (110) 90 I
7-9. (987) 789 D
10-12. (15) 3 I
13. >
14. <
15. >
16. <
17. =
18. =
19. >
20. <
21. 6
22. 2
23. odd
24. 200p
25. 5000 g
26. 1020 ml
27. 300 cm
28. 250
29. 540
30. 390
31. 26
32. 4 P
33. O
34. 10
35. 16
36. 70G
37. 39
38. 30
39. 25
40. 36

1. M
2. O
3. 6
4. 7
5. 11
6. 3
7. 30
8. 32
9. 80
10. 70
11. 100
12. 110
13. □□□□
14. ◯◯◯◯◯
15. 4 o'clock
16. 12
17. 11
18. 12
19. 12
20. 90^0
21. 45
22. 44
23. 59
24. 67
25. 74
26. 4
27. 5
28. 15
29. 42
30. 81
31. 1
32. 3
33. $5x$
34. 21
35. 80
36. 820
37. 11
38. 8
39. 4
40. 5

1. 2
2. 4
3. 3
4. 4
5. 6
6. Hane & Jim
7-8. Jake
9. Sam
10. Jake
11. 19 hours
12-13.  7.20

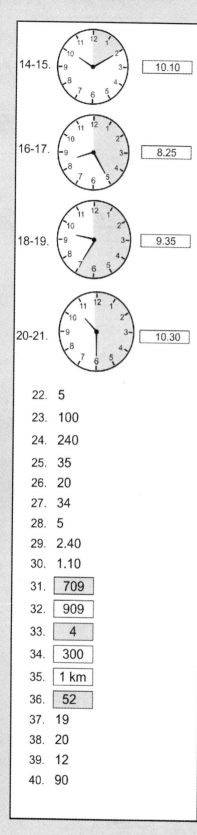

14-15. 10.10

16-17. 8.25

18-19. 9.35

20-21. 10.30

22. 5
23. 100
24. 240
25. 35
26. 20
27. 34
28. 5
29. 2.40
30. 1.10
31. 709
32. 909
33. 4
34. 300
35. 1 km
36. 52
37. 19
38. 20
39. 12
40. 90

TEST PAPER -6

1. 660 ml
2. 330 ml
3. 440 ml
4. 220 ml
5. 800 ml
6. 400 ml
7. 120 ml
8. 60 ml
9. Squash   Ice-Cream
10. Honey
11. 32
12. 14D
13. 50U
14. 10ef
15. 10 Years
16. 42
17. 27
18. 8
19. 4
20. 9
21. 7
22. 10
23. 11
24. 15
25. 40
26. 64
27. >
28. =
29. <
30. >
31. 657
32. 200
33. 2
34. 6
35. 2
36. 10
37. 10
38. 25
39. 8
40. 36

TEST PAPER -7

1. 50
2. 20
3. 28 cm
4. 24 cm
5. 12 cm
6. 35 cm
7. 5
8. 80
9. 40
10. 30
11. 80 cm
12. 25
13. 12
14. 50p
15. £1
16. 972
17. 279
18. 940
19. 409
20. 810
21. 108
22. Six hundred and thirty five
23. Five hundred and six
24. Eight hundred and ninety
25. Three hundred and five
26. 300
27. 499
28. 80

29.

30.

31. 7645
32. 998
33. $\frac{1}{2}$
34. cm
35. 5062
36. yes
37. no
38. no
39. 16
40. 125

TEST PAPER -8

1. 6	21. 109
2. 3	22. 89
3. 2	23. 18
4. 12	24. F
5. 2	25. 4x5
6. 1	26. △
7. 8	27. £ 9.72
8. 0 or no	28. 5.90 kg
9. 1	29. 7.99 ml
10. 18	30. 983
11. 6	31. 18:15
12. 24	32. 12
13. 333	33. g
14. 905	34. 101
15. 8	35. 1983
16. 20	36. 6023
17. 5	37. 632
18. 49	38. 200
19. 70	39. 509
20. 25	40. 225

TEST PAPER -9

1. 6
2. 5
3. G, H, B
4. I, J
5. D, F
6. A, C, E
7. $\frac{1}{2}$
8. 29
9. 4
10. 108
11. 19
12. 630
13. 50
14. 60
15. 20 cm
16. 3

17. 8
18. 5
19. 7
20. 20
21. 60
22. 40
23. 54
24. 42
25. 30
26. 585
27. 9
28. North
29. West
30. 7.50 am
31. 900
32. 07:45
33. 10
34. ml
35. 110
36. 2,910
37. 3
38. 1
39. 1
40. 2

TEST PAPER -10

1. $x_5 y_3$
2. $x_2 y_4$
3. $x_5 y_5$
4. $x_1 y_3$
5. y_1

x_1	x_2	x_3	x_4	x_5	x_6

6. 201
7. 156
8. 432
9. 62
10. 999
11. 30
12. 20
13. 40

14. 35
15. 30
16. 5
17. 35
18. 75
19. 30
20. 70
21. 95

22-28.

Odd	5	15	25	35	45
Even	10	20	30	40	50

29. 5
30. 6
31. 2000
32. 120
33. 10 x
34. 28
35. 4
36. 9.10 am
37. 5
38. 0
39. 5
40. 0

TEST PAPER -11

1. Football	17. >
2. 15	18. <
3. 5	19-20. 1, 18
4. Cycling	21-22. 6, 7
5. Football	23-24. 5, 12
6. Cricket	25-26. 10,11
7. 5	27. Cube
8. 15	28. 120p or £ 1.20
9. 10	
10. 30	29. 60p or £ 0.60
11. 20	
12. 25	30. 240p or £ 2.40
13. <	
14. >	31. Spoon
15. <	32. 405
16. >	

33.

34. 7th

35. 7th

36. 18:00

37. 12

38. 11

39. 10

40. 11

TEST PAPER -12

1. 6.00 am
2. 5
3. 9.00 am
4. 16
5. 40
6. 2
7. 10
8. 35
9. 30
10. 12
11. 6
12. 70
13. 65
14. 12
15. £ 7.78
16. £ 6.21
17. £ 4.44
18. £ 6.15
19. 3
20. $\frac{1}{4}$
21. $\frac{1}{2}$
22. $\frac{3}{4}$
23. $\frac{1}{2}$
24. $\frac{1}{3}$

25-26.

27-28.

29-30.

31. 900
32. 4
33. 300 g
34. 1500
35. 2
36. 5
37. 392
38. 264
39. 405
40. 564

TEST PAPER -13

1. 4
2. Cartoons
3. 6
4. 2
5. 10
6. 28
7. >
8. <
9. =
10. 4
11. E
12. 8
13. E
14. 11
15. o
16. 17
17. o

18-23.

24. 220
25. 10
26. 40

27. £ 1.90
28. 60
29. 11.50 am
30. 4
31. m
32. 10
33. 6
34. 150
35. 2
36. 0
37. 0
38. 10
39. 981
40. 10

TEST PAPER -14

1. a, b
2. burger
3. C
4. i
5-8. d, e, h, i
9. e
10-11. j, l
12. $\frac{1}{2}$
13. $\frac{1}{4}$
14. $\frac{2}{3}$
15. $\frac{1}{3}$
16. one third
17. 2
18. 4
19. 3
20. 6
21. 6
22. 3
23. 9
24. 3
25. 4
26. 12
27. 57
28. 7
29. (figure)
30. (figure)
31. 14
32. $\frac{C}{6}$
33. Circle
34. (figure)
35. 26
36. $\frac{3}{4}$
37. 90
38. 30
39. 50
40. 20

TEST PAPER -15

1-10. 9 210 **80** 81 210 80
L O N D O N

11. LONDON
12. $\frac{1}{6}$
13. 9
14. V
15. X

16. 4
17. 10
18. 3
19. 2
20. 16
21. 18
22. 25
23. 500 cm or 5m
24. 457
25. 754
26. 609
27. 960
28. 8
29. £ 3.00
30. 680 cm
31. 989
32. 8 cm
33. 3
34. 10
35. 205
36. 520
37. 7
38. 9
39. 0
40. 0

TEST PAPER -16

1-2. CIRCLE
3-4. CONE
5-6. CUBOID
7-8. SPHERE

9. £ 12.00
10. 1 m
11. 5 ml
12. 80
13. 100
14. 400
15.
16.
17.
18. 400
19. 7
20. 700
21. 6
22. 10
23. 90
24. 28
25. 32
26. 576
27. 165
28. 2, 7
29. 50, 7
30. 709
31. 1026
32. 200 ml
33. 25 cm^2
34. 15
35. 1400
36. 50
37. 50
38. 3
39. 5
40. 10

TEST PAPER -17

1. 200
2. C
3. 300
4. 100
5. $\frac{1}{2}$
6. 600
7. 200
8. 1200
9. 7.10 am
10. 6.15 am
11. 15
12. 60
13. 75
14. 39
15. 13
16. 6
17. 2
18. 4
19. -
20. x
21. ÷
22. -
23. ÷
24. x
25. $\frac{2}{5}$
26. 999
27. 1.20
28.
29.
30. 8
31. 9210
32. 200 g
33. M
34. 400 g
35. 15
36. 60
37. 36
38. 11
39. 81
40. 17

TEST PAPER -18

1-4.

Multiples of 5	5	10	15	20	25	30	35	40

5-12.

13. 4
14. 2
15. 2
16. 8
17. 3
18. 5
19. $\frac{2}{5}$
20. 205
21. 08:15
22. 9.50 pm
23. $\frac{1}{4}, \frac{1}{2}, \frac{3}{4}$
24. 42
25.
26.
27.

(ix)

28.	29	35.	1
29.	19	36.	10 am
30.	16	37.	68
31.	333	38.	40
32.	10	39.	60
33.	13	40.	50
34.	12 cm		

TEST PAPER -19

1. E
2. W
3. C or E
4. M or W
5. S
6. C
7. L
8. NE
9. E
10. 70
11. 3.10
12. 72
13. 3
14. 6
15. 15
16. 16 cm
17. 162
18. 62
19. 6.20
20. 16.2
21. 8
22. 6
23. 2 and 3
24. 3 and 7
25. 3 and 5
26. 1 and 25
27. 6
28. 60

29.

30.

31. 120°C
32. 320 cm
33. 56
34.

35.	8
36.	5
37.	80
38.	9
39.	90
40.	49

TEST PAPER -20

1.	B	22.	200
2.	F	23.	1400
3.	E	24.	5
4.	A	25.	400
5.	G	26.	N
6.	D	27.	24
7.	C	28.	30
8.	H	29.	East or E
9.	F	30.	70
10.	A	31.	$\frac{1}{2}$
11-12.	D and E	32.	13
13.	400	33.	Acute angle
14.	300		
15.	6	34.	J
16.	30	35.	16
17.	40	36.	15
18.	£ 5.00	37.	2
19.	£ 6.56	38.	6
20.	24	39.	4
21.	198	40.	9